Literature of Developing Nations for Students, Volume 2

Staff

Series Editors: Elizabeth Bellalouna, Michael L. LaBlanc, and Ira Mark Milne.

Contributing Editors: Elizabeth Bodenmiller, Reginald Carlton, Anne Marie Hacht, Jennifer Smith.

Managing Editor: Dwayne Hayes.

Research: Victoria B. Cariappa, *Research Team Manager.* Maureen Eremic, Barb McNeil, Cheryl Warnock, *Research Specialists.* Andy Malonis, *Technical Training Specialist.* Barbara Leevy, Tamara Nott, Tracie A. Richardson, Robert Whaley, *Research Associates.* Scott Floyd, Nicodemus Ford, Sarah Genik, Timothy Lehnerer, *Research Assistants.*

Permissions: Maria Franklin, *Permissions*

Manager. Margaret A. Chamberlain, Edna Hedblad, *Permissions Specialists.* Erin Bealmear, Shalice Shah-Caldwell, Sarah Tomasek, *Permissions Associates.* Debra Freitas, Julie Juengling, Mark Plaza, *Permissions Assistants.*

Manufacturing: Mary Beth Trimper, *Manager, Composition and Electronic Prepress.* Evi Seoud, *Assistant Manager, Composition Purchasing and Electronic Prepress.* Stacy Melson, *Buyer.*

Imaging and Multimedia Content Team: Randy Bassett, *Image Database Supervisor.* Robert Duncan, Dan Newell, *Imaging Specialists.* Pamela A. Reed, *Imaging Coordinator.* Dean Dauphinais, Robyn V. Young, *Senior Image Editors.* Kelly A. Quin, *Image Editor.*

Product Design Team: Kenn Zorn, *Product Design Manager.* Pamela A. E. Galbreath, *Senior Art Director.* Michael Logusz, *Graphic Artist.*

Library of Congress Cataloging-in-Publication Data

Literature of developing nations for students / Michael L. LaBlanc, Elizabeth Bellalouna, Ira Mark Milne, editors.
v.; cm.
Includes bibliographical references and index.
Contents: v. 1. A-L — v. 2. M-Z.
ISBN 0-7876-4928-7 (set: alk. paper) — ISBN 0-7876-4929-5 (vol. 1) — ISBN 0-7876-4930-9 (vol. 2)
1. Fiction—Stories, plots, *etc.* 2. Fiction—History and criticism. 3. Developing countries—Literatures

—History and criticism. [1. Fiction—Stories, plots, *etc.* 2. Fiction—History and criticism. 3. Developing countries—Literatures—History and criticism.] I. LaBlanc, Michael L. II. Bellalouna, Elizabeth. III. Milne, Ira Mark. IV. Title.
PN3326 .L58 2000
809'.891724—dc21
00-056023

Copyright Notice

Since this page cannot legibly accommodate all copyright notices, the acknowledgments constitute an extension of the copyright notice.

While every effort has been made to secure permission to reprint material and to ensure the reliability of the information presented in this publication, Gale neither guarantees the accuracy of the data contained herein nor assumes any responsibility for errors, omissions, or discrepancies. Gale accepts no payment for listing; and inclusion in the publication of any organization, agency, institution, publication, service, or individual does not imply endorsement of the editors or publisher. Errors brought to the attention of the publisher and verified to the satisfaction of the publisher will be corrected in future editions.

This publication is a creative work fully protected by all applicable copyright laws, as well as by misappropriation, trade secret, unfair competition, and other applicable laws. The authors and editors of this work have added value to the underlying factual material herein through one or more of the following: unique and original selection, coordination, expression, arrangement, and classification of the information. All rights to this publication will be vigorously defended.

Copyright © 2000
Gale Group, Inc.
27500 Drake Road
Farmington Hills, MI 48331-3535

All rights reserved including the right of reproduction in whole or in part in any form.

ISBN 0-7876-4930-9

Printed in the United States of America.

10 9 8 7 6 5 4 3 2 1

The Time of the Hero

Mario Vargas Llosa 1962

Introduction

One of the greatest Latin American novelists of the twentieth century, Mario Vargas Llosa belongs to a group of writers who brought Latin American fiction out of the regionalist doldrums of the nineteenth century to the attention of the world. This group includes Jorge Luis Borges, Gabriel García Márquez, Julio Cortazar, and Carlos Fuentes. Vargas Llosa, sometimes referred to as the national conscience of Peru, has made a career out of adapting personal and historical events, without bothering about accuracy, to the novel using highly sophisticated techniques of nonlinearity and multiple viewpoint.

His first novel, winner of the Premio Biblioteca Breve (1962) and Premio de la Critica Espanola (1963), *La ciudad y los perros* (literally "the city and the dogs" but published in English as *The Time of the Hero)* made use of his own experience at the Leoncio Prado Academy. The novel was so accurate in its portraiture of the academy that the academy's authorities burned 1000 copies and condemned the book as a plan by Ecuador to denigrate Peru. Such a reception guaranteed the book's sales but its content made it the greatest Latin American novel of adolescence: It is the story of young Peruvian males in their transition to manhood.

The Time of the Hero tells a tale of murder: a squealing cadet must be silenced by a gang called The Circle. The reasons given by The Circle, as well as the rationalization of the authorities to excuse the death as an accident, reveal the process of forming boys into men in a world dominated by the military. The academy does not teach fundamentals; it teaches boys how to exist in hierarchical command-structures and to never, ever squeal. The main characters suffer through a military academy but minor characters portray a non-military route. Although a microcosm of Peruvian society, the novel's themes are universal: masculinity, secrecy, and the military.

Author Biography

Although born in Arequipa, Peru, in 1936, Vargas Llosa spent his early boyhood with his mother, Dora Llosa Ureta, in Cochabamba, Bolivia, where his grandfather was the Peruvian consul. Vargas Llosa attended a series of schools and led a normal middle-class boy's life until his parents reunited and his father, Ernesto Vargas Maldonaldo, discovered his talent for writing poetry. Fearing for the boy's masculinity, Ernesto moved the family to Lima and sent the boy, in 1950, to attend Leoncio Prado Academy. His two years at the academy formed the basis for a novella as well as his famous first novel, *The Time of the Hero*.

His first work, however, was a three-act play published in 1952 while finishing high school in Piura. For the next few years, Vargas Llosa published short stories in Peruvian literary reviews. He also coedited several journals and attended San Marcos University in Lima where he took courses in literature and law. In 1955, he caused a minor family scandal when he married Julia Urquidi —his aunt. They divorced in 1964.

In 1958, he left for Europe and lived for varying periods in Paris, England, the U.S., and Spain. While in France, Vargas Llosa worked on the manuscript that would become *The Time of the Hero*. This became his first novel in 1962 and won two major awards establishing him as a major Latin

American novelist—a stature that would be cemented with his second novel, *The Green House* (1966). During this time, in 1959, he completed a dissertation on Gabriel García Márquez's fiction at the University of Madrid. Also during this time, Vargas Llosa was an intellectual spokesman for revolutionary movements throughout Latin America. This advocacy period ended in 1971 when his criticism of the censorship of artists in Cuba caused him to be ostracized by the Latin American Left. He married Patricia (a cousin) in 1965 and they had three children: Alvaro, Gonzalo, and Morgana.

Vargas Llosa returned to Peru in 1974 and seven years later, *The War of the End of the World* announced his abandonment of socialism. He began espousing free-market democracy and anti-authoritarian liberalism in Peru. He turned down the post of prime minister in the early 1980s to concentrate on writing but the government's plan to nationalize the banks of Peru in 1987 forced him to stand up for his beliefs and protest the plan. Vargas Llosa quickly gained supporters and the government backed down. Fired by this victory, his supporters formed Fredemo, a political party, to champion the ideas of free-market democracy and individual liberty. Fredemo formed a coalition, Liberty Movement, with two other parties. Together, they nominated Vargas Llosa as their presidential candidate. In 1988, opinion polls showed Vargas Llosa well ahead of his rival, Alberto Fujimori, by more than 2 to 1. However, his support gradually eroded and Vargas Llosa lost. He reflected on this political experience in *A Fish in the Water.*

Not long after the election, Vargas Llosa returned to Spain, where he accepted citizenship. However, he currently spends his time in London.

Plot Summary

The Circle

The Time of the Hero opens at night during a meeting of The Circle—a gang of four cadets in their final year of the Leoncio Prado Academy led by the Jaguar. Their clubhouse is "the windowless latrine" and they are rolling the dice to see who will steal the answers to the chemistry exam. This criminal act sets off a violent chain reaction although The Circle intended only to pass an important exam a mere two months before graduation. Cava, a peasant, rolled the four, meaning he must make arrangements on behalf of The Circle with those cadets on duty to grant him anonymous passage to the academic building. This is easily granted and Cava goes off into the night while Boa and Curly, relieved by the roll of the die, go off to bed.

Later that night, while the Poet and the Slave (forced to take Jaguar's place), who are members of the same section as The Circle, are on patrol. Cava goes forth to steal the exam. While the Poet engages Lt. Huarina in a strange metaphysical discussion away from his proper post, the Slave observes Cava crossing to the academic building. While breaking into the building, Cava accidentally breaks a windowpane he had just painfully removed. As Boa later says, "You have to be stupid to do that" and scared. Cava, as a peasant, was susceptible to both. Grabbing the exam and scooping the shards of glass into his pocket, Cava runs back to the barracks.

The Slave

When the exam's theft is discovered, those who were on patrol that night are confined to barracks until the responsible party confesses or someone squeals. The Slave, whose life has been "sheer hell" due to the abuse rained on him by the section and particularly The Circle, had rarely been free of confinement. Most recently, he sent the Poet to Teresa's house to make apologies on his behalf for missing a date. Because of the exam theft, the Slave has been confined again. The Slave asks the Poet to write a letter to Teresa but the Poet refuses. The Slave, in desperation, decides to squeal. Among the cadets, squealing is the worst crime to commit against fellow cadets. However, as Jaguar reveals at the end of the novel, squealing can be justified if done out of revenge for a comrade but not for the sake of getting a pass. The Slave, fed up with being kept from seeing Teresa, reasons that he has everything to gain by squealing on his tormentors. With such motives, the Slave squeals on Cava to Lt. Huarina and receives a pass.

Unknown to the Slave, the Poet—who had written letters to Teresa for the Slave—decides to take Teresa for himself. Too cowardly to admit this to the Slave, he simultaneously befriends the Slave while refusing to write letters for him. The Poet tries to get the Slave to stop being cowardly but the real coward is the Poet. As the Poet tells Teresa, during the Slave's time of anguish "he thought I was his friend" but the Poet was really stealing his girlfriend. However, Teresa makes it quite clear she never viewed the Slave as her boyfriend.

When Cava's court-martial becomes expulsion, the Jaguar "almost went crazy afterward but not on account of the peasant, just himself." Since the Jaguar organized his year against hazing when they were first-years, he had become the undisputed ringleader. Therefore, to squeal on any scheme of his was to betray the Jaguar himself. He therefore gathers with his remaining circle to figure out who squealed. But Jaguar already knows; like an animal, he can smell it. He decides to cleanse his section of its weak element once and for all. His Darwinian act stems from loyalty to the group and himself.

The Cover-Up

While on a training exercise, the Slave—who happens to be directly in front of the Jaguar—is shot. Enraged by this act and feeling guilty at having made a move on the Slave's girl, the Poet spills the beans to Lt. Gamboa—he reveals the way the cadets break rules against drinking, smoking, gambling, and sneaking out as well as his theory that The Circle took its revenge. The Slave, says the Poet, did not accidentally shoot himself as the official story academy officials are telling parents says (the doctors made a strictly medical report and neglected to mention that "there's isn't any question about it, he got shot from behind"), but Jaguar shot him. Lt. Gamboa believes him and raids the barracks of the first section to find evidence to substantiate the Poet's claims about rule infraction but no evidence against the Jaguar.

Angered by all the trouble, the Colonel intercedes in the investigation. During the locker searches, all the pornographic writings of the Poet come to light. With these stories in hand, the Colonel blackmails the Poet; if the Poet will withdraw the charge and be a perfect angel, the writings will be burnt. The Colonel then, by referencing the Poet's fantastic writing, tells him that clearly his imagination ran away with him and he dreamed up the conspiracy. Seeing he has no support and no evidence, the Poet agrees to withdraw the charge. Before being released, he is mistakenly imprisoned with Jaguar. They fight and the Poet gets the worst of it. After being ordered silent by Lt. Gamboa, the cadets return to the barracks. Along the way, the Poet begins to doubt himself because the Jaguar appears genuinely surprised that it was the Slave who squealed on Cava. Thus, everyone can believe the official story which labels the Slave's death accidental.

Useless Objectives

Lt. Gamboa, who acted on the Poet's information and turned the barracks upside down during an investigation of rule infraction, is transferred to an out-of-the-way post. Just before he goes, Jaguar confesses to him. He is motivated by self-revelation—the entire fifth year blames the Jaguar for Lt. Gamboa's crackdown and they shun him. Jaguar accepts this because he refuses to squeal on the Poet, but he realizes how the Slave must have felt. Lt. Gamboa tells him to forget the whole thing because nobody wants to know: to clear up the death of the Slave would be an attempt at a "useless objective." By this Lt. Gamboa means that, just as in war, when an enemy surrenders you do not kill him because that would be bad economics: "it would be easier to bring Arana back to life than to convince the army it's made an error." Jaguar's epiphany includes the realization that the world of loyalty he created among the cadets was a false and fickle one.

The end of the novel is fraught with ambiguity. The cadets graduate and return home to forget all about the academy. At this point, the unidentified fourth narrator reveals himself as the Jaguar: the legitimate suitor of Teresa who struggled on the streets as an orphan. Jaguar marries Teresa and finds a steady job. The Poet, meanwhile, still melancholy about the academy, chooses someone from the middle class. He intends to marry her after he gets an engineering degree in the U.S. In the end, both the Poet and the Jaguar marvel at how normal life went on without them, as if the horror of the academy means nothing. Moreover, although their insight might have led them to change their views of society, each happily resumes his designated place; the Jaguar becomes a lowly functionary, while the Poet takes his place in the upper class. Worse, the Poet, using a metaphor repeated throughout the novel, "could remember many of the events as if they were a motion picture, and for days at a time he could avoid thinking of the Slave."

Characters

Mr. Arana

Mr. Arana differs from Alberto's father only slightly. He does not treat his wife well, abandons her for stretches of time, and has many girlfriends. He is an absent father to Ricardo, the Slave, and blames his wife for Ricardo's fault. When Ricardo has been shot and lies dying in the hospital, Mr. Arana moans to Alberto about the challenge he has had to face in making Ricardo a man: "It hasn't been easy to make a man out of him. He's my only son." Mr. Arana wants to believe the Academy did him good, that it undid all that his wife and Aunt Adeline did to emasculate young Ricardo. Mr. Arana does everything but consider his role in Ricardo's upbringing, especially his failure to ever appreciate Ricardo. In fact, Mr. Arana constantly insulted Ricardo as if he were not there, saying, "he acts like a girl." Mr. Arana represents the worst kind of father.

Ricardo Arana

Ricardo, in terms of the *machismo* of Peruvian society, is a degenerate. Faced with the bravest boy in grade school, "he was not afraid...all he felt was a complete discouragement and resignation." From this moment on, Ricardo adopted a humble and subservient attitude and employed passive-aggressive strategies with his father and other macho performers. This personality wins him the designation of Slave by the Jaguar, who makes use of his natural subservience.

Ricardo's inability to play silly games and to feel fear of his fellow humans as well as his desire to protect his mother from his misogynistic father mark him as someone destined to die. Ricardo makes men aware of the fallibility of their *machismo* behavior. Thus, Ricardo carries incredible symbolic weight and can be interpreted according to many patterns. Ricardo represents the existentialist stranger, the man who speaks the truth in Plato's cave. As in that parable, he must die. Ricardo can be read as a Christ figure who dies for the sins of the boys at the hands of their high priest. His death serves as a possible means of salvation for those willing to reflect. However, Ricardo's death does not bring salvation but allows the boys to continue to play at being men.

Arrospide

Arrospide, a rich white kid from Miraflores (like Alberto), intends to survive the Academy with good marks and in good standing with his peers. Based on these goals, Arrospide willingly accepts the thankless role of Brigadier of the first section for all three years. He allows The Circle liberty and simply goes with the flow. In the end, he leads the coup against the Jaguar with relish. By destroying the Jaguar, whether or not the rumor Curly started is true, Arrospide becomes the leader of the first section in name and spirit just in time for graduation.

The Boa

See Valdivieso

Porfitio Cava

"Cava had been born and brought up in the mountains, cold weather was nothing new to him; it was fear that was giving him goose pimples." The fear stalking Cava is the fear of failure both to please the Jaguar and to survive the academy; it is the fear of being unable to handle a situation forced upon him. If he doesn't survive the academy, he is destined to live the life of a peasant. If he does survive, he hopes to climb the social ladder however slightly through a career in the military. Fate is against him in the most iconographic sense—he rolls the dice and lands a "four." "Get going," the Jaguar commands. Cava must steal the answers to the upcoming chemistry exam for the other three members of The Circle and for whoever else wants to buy them.

Cava, an Indian, wins respect by being a part of The Circle. Thus, even an avowed racist like the Boa forgives him for being Indian and befriends him. Cava plays the role of The Circle's peddler in the section. He arranges the selling of items stolen from other cadets in other sections to fellow cadets who want to pass inspection. Cava has a special hatred for the French teacher, Mr. Fontana. Consequently, Cava makes French class hell for Fontana. He thinks Fontana is gay and relentlessly disrupts class. The Boa and the other cadets both approve of and follow Cava's lead.

Curly

A member of The Circle who partakes in the gang bangs and acts of bestiality described by the Boa. He witnesses the Jaguar's vow, "if I get screwed, everybody gets screwed." Upon this basis, the section labels the Jaguar a squealer when Gamboa ransacks the barracks for misdemeanors.

Alberto Fernandez

One of the protagonists, Alberto, earned his nickname when he began writing letters and pornographic stories for money. The Poet shares his origination from a comfortable white middle-class family in Miraflores with the brigadier, Arrospide. However, inside the academy, such a background does not mean much. Only the esteem of one's fellow cadets brings merit. Along with being a narrator of his own life and contemporary events, the Poet brings about the major event of the novel by underhandedly pursuing his friend's girl. While he does not find Teresa beautiful, the Poet admires her intelligence and enjoys the attention she gives him. It is the attention a poor girl gives to anyone sporting the equipage of a higher station in society.

The Poet, as the most conscious and articulate character, receives the most scrutiny because he is the most revealed. Consequently, the evidence never substantiates his claim on reliability and masculinity. This uncertainty begins with his introduction when he confusingly attempts to mislead and seek advice from a man he does not respect, Lt. Huarina. Again and again, the Poet will behave in a manner that clashes with the code of honor and *machismo* he is supposed to be learning. For example, real men brag about sexual exploits that they actually have. Instead, both in his pornographic writing and when he talks about the prostitute, Golden Toes, "no one suspected that he knew about [Golden Toes] because he repeated anecdotes he had been told and invented all kinds of lurid stories." Pained adolescence and the demands of military *machismo* excuse such lying behavior, but for the Poet they become a habit that spills into civilian life.

At his duplicitous worst, the Poet never corrects the Slave in his idea that the two of them are friends. Instead, the Poet tries to make a man of the Slave and hides the truth about his relations with Teresa. This act of cowardice haunts him when he is forced to console the Slave's father with lies about how great the Slave was. Finally, with such a compromised integrity and tortured by doubt, he cannot challenge Jaguar using truth as an instrument. Indeed, Jaguar easily dupes him with a story just as the Colonel blackmailed the Poet with his pornographic stories. The Poet represents a theory of literature—stories change and make up reality until it is difficult to discern what is real and what is story.

Like the Slave, the Poet exists as an existential stranger. He never entirely bends to the wishes of The Circle and they punish him by denying access to the exam answers. Instead of bending to those around him, the Poet deludes himself and others with his stories and letters. He assumes the role of the fool in Jaguar's court or his Cave. He produces the fantasies that distract and amuse the cadets and, in return, the Poet is unharmed. He serves his purpose but it is without purpose. When Alberto finds purpose—love, friendship, truth—it is too late because he has cried wolf too many times with his stories. In fact, Alberto is not even sure if he believes that Jaguar killed Ricardo.

Lieutenant Gamboa

Lieutenant Gamboa represents the ideal soldier. All the cadets stand in awe of him. He is their role model. His notion of justice and military propriety is based on the book of regulations that he has memorized. His attempt to enforce those regulations when the Poet squeals brings him exile in Juliaca.

Flaco Higueras

Flaco, known as Skinny, is a thief who helps Jaguar help his mother with household expenses. Skinny also teaches Jaguar how to survive in the world of *machismo.*

Lieutenant Remigio Huarina

Among the cadets and officers, Huarina fosters little respect. "He was small and weak, his voice when he gave commands made everyone laugh." In addition, his punishments are arbitrary; Huarina invented "the punishment lottery" by which cadets are randomly punished depending on where they stand in formation. In the black and white world of the military, nobody respects arbitrary gray.

When the Slave decides to stand up to the world, he goes to Huarina and squeals on Cava. Huarina seizes the information with enthusiasm hoping that he will win some respect. Huarina gains in standing and represents the classic situation of the victory of the undeserving. Gamboa, the man with the most integrity, gains exile—Huarina, a promotion.

The Jaguar

Central and South American ranchers mistakenly view the largest member of the American cat family, the endangered jaguar (once honored as a god among pre-Columbian Peruvians), as a pest. They believe that the jaguar eats their cattle, scientific evidence to the contrary notwithstanding. A forest and savanna creature, the jaguar wears a coat ranging from yellow to rust red with black rosettes. The jaguar is a fitting namesake for the story's most powerful and mysterious personality.

The Jaguar works in the shadows as his stalking of Cava shows from the start. Cava, when returning from his hunt, sees "a dark shape loom[ing] up in front of him." The Jaguar, with "big pale feet with long dirty toenails" and hands "like two white claws," takes Cava's prey, the exam answers. Such characteristic actions prompt Boa to say "the devil must have a face like the Jaguar's, the same kind of smile, the same sharp horns." But it is the Jaguar's laugh that really gets people.

The Jaguar's effort to make men out of his fellow cadets is done, as all evil intentions are, for his own benefit. Therefore, he represents the man-making tool that parents believe resides inside the academy. However, the Jaguar—and the parents behind him—never realize that boys like Alberto and Ricardo must act for themselves, find their own identities and their own manhood. It was the Jaguar's paternal impatience, more than any thing else, that made him confess to being the cause of Ricardo's death. According to the Jaguar, "we" all killed him.

Marcela

Like Helena, the young woman who dumps and humiliates Alberto, Marcela is a member of Alberto's social class. Cementing the idea that Alberto willingly imitates his Don Juan-esque father, Marcela is an anagram for the name of

Alberto's mother, Carmela. Marcela signifies that Alberto will occupy an important position in Peruvian society like his parents and his grandparents.

The Negro

See Vallano

The Poet

See Alberto Fernandez

Skinny

See Flaco Higueras

The Slave

See Ricardo Arana

Teresa

Within the masculine discourse of the barracks, there are two types of woman. The first, Golden Toes, is the whore upon whom the aspiring soldier can practice his lust. The other is the virgin. Teresa represents the virgin who is to be protected in times of war and maintained by a proper husband in times of peace. The Slave, the Jaguar, and the Poet compete for the love of Teresa. Thus, although she simply goes to school, works, and cleans house, Teresa is a major moving force in the novel and in the world of boys. Teresa also allows for an examination of class in Peruvian society; the Jaguar wins her hand at the end, thus allowing him to move up the social ladder and occupy a position as a clerk in a bank.

Valdivieso

In South America, the largest of the boa or boidae, the anaconda, are known to measure twenty feet. Legends have grown up about boas and the people of the Amazon basin are wary of the creatures. The character Boa is named for this South American reptile. A snake can also symbolize the phallus. The Boa, who has a "huge body, a deep voice, a shock of greasy hair over a narrow face," embodies the animal nature of young males and their awakening sexual preoccupations. He always wins the puerile physical contests the first section holds to pass the time—especially masturbatory races judged by Paulino. In terms of the novel, the Boa represents the perfect cadet: his irreproachable loyalty and physical abilities makes him an ideal soldier; his lackluster intelligence enables him to follow orders; and his genuine love of life make him a pleasurable person to live with. Even though he is a narrator, beyond the Boa's reflections on life in the Academy he does not move the plot. Instead, he tells readers about previous actions The Circle, of which he is a prominent member, has choreographed and he also recounts the physical exploits of other cadets.

The Boa expresses the racism of Peruvian society through his comments on Indians and peasants. He tells how he had to make an exception for Cava—an Indian from the mountains—with great difficulty. Otherwise, the Boa regards blacks, Indians, or mixed breeds as inferior. The Boa, as his name suggests, is an animal. He has sex with chickens and then roasts them. He cruelly manipulates a dog's affections and even maims the animal for disturbing him during an inspection. Just like a snake, he never quite accepts the Jaguar as his master and often fantasizes about killing him—stealthily as would a snake. However, the Jaguar has tamed him as a charmer tames a snake, using the tune of violence. The Boa, at his most eloquent, recollects the fights The Circle has engaged in with the Jaguar at the lead.

Vallano

Unlike Cava, Vallano, a black cadet, cannot escape the overt racism of the lighter-hued Peruvians. They call him "The Negro" and describe him in stereotypical fashion, saying, "like all Negroes, you can tell it from his eyes, what eyes, what fear, what jumping around" or, the oft-repeated, "who can trust a Negro." With such a name, a physical name not unlike the animal names, it is not surprising that Vallano is a sympathizer of The Circle although he is not a member. Still, they recognize the Negro as the only "real" student. For this reason, the Poet deals with him as often as possible. The Poet, after the Jaguar turns him down, offers a few letters for a certain number of points on the chemistry exam. During the exam, Vallano is the only student described as working through the questions.

Vallano makes a huge contribution to the culture of the Fifth Section when he brings a pornographic story back from town. *Eleodora's Pleasures* becomes the favorite reading of every member of the section. When Vallano started the story out he found himself out of business because the Poet started selling his own stories. From that moment on, pornographic tales become an intrinsic and sophisticated component of life in the barracks.

Themes

Masculinity

According to Lt. Gamboa, half the boys are sent to the academy "so they won't be gangsters… and the other half, so they won't turn out to be fairies. It's their parents' fault." Gamboa's comment leads to a discussion about the difference between soldiers and cadets. Soldiers can be physically beaten until they are so civilized an Indian only appears to be Indian. Cadets, which cannot be so abused, are not quite so accomplished but they do learn one thing: being a man depends on whether a boy is s--------- or he s----------. In military terms, the ultimate sign of manhood is murder. However, his parents determine the degree of a boy's success either by letting him grow up—like Tico or Skinny —or telling him to become a man. Towards that end, parents send their boys to an academy where the boys must negotiate a paradox. They are expected to be soldier-like men but they are not soldiers, they are not killers.

Topics for Further Study

- The initiation rituals described in the novel are also known by the term "hazing." Research the role of hazing in neighborhoods, gangs, boarding schools, fraternities, or military academies. What is hazing and how does it differ depending on setting, if at all? Why is this traditional practice under scrutiny? What are the legal issues? Do you think hazing is simply a part of growing up and that the death rate is unavoidable?

- How many levels of masculinity are there in the novel? How many levels of race? Compare the multiplicity of hierarchical levels in Peruvian society to the structure of the U.S.

- William Faulkner looms behind the Latin American Boom. Compare Faulkner's *Light in August* to *The Time of the Hero*. How, for example, has Vargas Llosa drawn from Faulkner and with what results?

- Given the preoccupation with sex that the adolescent boys have throughout the novel, reflect on the implications of the opening citation from Sartre on gender.

- Research the debate in America over gays in the military. How has the debate changed perceptions of masculinity?

- Research the role of the U.S. in the manufacturing of military regimes throughout Latin America during the Cold War. For example, why do U.S. and Latin American political activists object to the U.S.'s School of the Americas? What sort of academy is it and what are the most likely accomplishments of its graduates?

The Slave does not succeed in becoming a man because the deck is stacked against him. He has a nearly Freudian relationship with his mother, indicated by his awareness of her kissing him on the lips: "Why does she kiss me on the mouth?" He learns the hard way that his parents are merely separated and suddenly sees "his mother and a man were...kissing." Slave, in undeclared rebellion, refuses to kiss his father. Later, he tries to defend his mother against being beat up. He loses and is unable to fight another man again; he is impotent. Such docility causes his father to send him to the military academy where he hopes they will make "a man out of him." His father blames the mother, declaring, "There's nothing like a woman to ruin a boy's life".

In contrast to the Slave, the Poet does not take his mother's side. He does kiss his father's cheek. Consequently, Poet's father acknowledges him: "He's a man now." Thereafter, Poet imitates his father's attitude toward his mother by neglecting her. The Jaguar is successful because he has no father to compete with and is acknowledged early on as a man. His aunt ensures his success as a man by sleeping with him—s---------other people is an essential component of being a man. Skinny helps by teaching Jaguar how to manipulate others and how to fight. All of this helps Jaguar be the man to teach his fellow cadets how to survive. He has only one more step to take: murder.

The Poet tries to help the Slave overcome his docility but instead reveals that what makes him most manly is fear. "But you're a soldier here whether you like it or not. And the thing in the army is to be real tough, to have guts... S---------them first before they s---------you. There isn't any other way. I don't like to be s---------." Being s--------can be literal—as with Boa's rape of chickens, dogs, and a first-year named "fatboy." But it is also metaphorical. The Jaguar's enslavement of Slave—the Slave does the Jaguar's work—is a form of emasculation.

Masculinity depends on acknowledgment by older men and women of one's manhood. It also depends on the stature a boy can hold among his fellow gang members. Except for Jaguar, the cadets are in an awkward position. Teresa's aunt echoes the commiseration of Lt. Gamboa: "The Academy! …I thought he was a man." However, one can beat that trap since "a man has to accept responsibility for his actions…" The recognition of the Jaguar's accomplishment will not come from the gang he formed; it must come from outside. He realizes that and confesses to Gamboa. He is not punished but freed to build a life with Teresa: the surest proof of manhood, the family.

Secrecy

Along with masculinity, secrecy is the most prevalent theme in the novel. From the start, the world of the cadets exists "in the uncertain glow" of a lightbulb. Secrecy is what allows the next generation to form: "The officers don't know anything about what goes on in the barracks." This is natural. Gamboa doesn't seem concerned about his lack of information or about their nicknames even though early in the novel he says, "I know them as if they were my own kids." However, as the

Poet continues to tell him what the cadets do in secret and how they exist, this concerns Gamboa. The level of secrecy that marks the culture of the barracks mirrors that of the thieves in Skinny's band. Secrecy maintains the foundation of group loyalty and the foundation of the Academy. Secrecy is supported with physical pressure and taunting.

The Jaguar, the focal point of secrecy, explains all of this to Gamboa. He explains it because he realizes that he no longer needs a group to sustain his personal identity but he does need the understanding of a very well-respected officer like Gamboa. Jaguar realizes this after Arrospide identifies him as a squealer: "You're a traitor, a coward…you don't even deserve to have us beat you up." Jaguar realizes there is no gratitude from the group he created. He tells Gamboa the ultimate secret, that he killed the Slave because the Slave was an insult to masculinity, to the section, and to him personally. In response, the exiled Gamboa—the only officer of integrity—sets Jaguar free. The secret is kept because they both know that if the secret were revealed to the Colonel, the Academy would be destroyed.

Friendship

Because of the masculine discourse wherein a man is the s---------or the s---------, the idea of friendship becomes charged with uneasiness and confusion. The intricacies of masculine loyalties betray the finer notions of what being a friend is all about. This begins with Alberto's reminiscences of his childhood. Having been invited to partake in soccer games, his recollections are a series of tales of bravado: broken windows, running from the authorities, having a girlfriend, or negotiating a steep cliff. At the academy, this intensifies. Boa defines friendship by fighting: defending the Jaguar, winning approval, and being tough. The Poet and Slave almost escape this cycle but the Poet, corrupted by barracks discourse, is too homophobic and full of subterfuge. Poet just wants Teresa.

The Slave admits that the Poet has won his confidence: "You're the only friend I've got...the only person I like to be with." Such an honest admission makes the Poet uneasy at several levels. Most immediately, it challenges the notions he holds about masculinity: "That sounds like the way a fairy says he's in love with somebody." But the Slave does not allow the discourse of the abusive barracks to intrude. Instead, he continues to be a friend—generous with himself and his cigarettes— and the Poet enjoys responding. Against his will, the Poet enjoys talking with the Slave without needing to perform with all the *machismo* required by Boa or Jaguar. However, the Poet has learned, from the Academy, that friendship must include pain and, perversely, he clings to this by not telling the Slave about stealing Teresa. Ironically, the only one hurt by the secret is the Poet.

Realizing the value of the Slave's gift, the Poet mourns him openly. Jaguar mourns him too, in his own way. Both young men have tasted genuine humanity in the Christ-like Slave. Poet admits all this to Teresa, proclaiming, "He was my friend." Worse than that, the Slave "thought I was his friend and I' was using him in the same way everyone else used him. The Slave gives self-knowledge to the Poet and to Jaguar. As a result, neither is the same nor are they able to run with the crowd.

Style

Narrative

Excepting a few geniuses—like Joanot Martorell and Victor Hugo whose *Les Miserables* Vargas Llosa read while attending the Leoncio Prado Academy—the novel before Flaubert and Faulkner, according to Vargas Llosa, is primitive. The novels of the nineteenth and early twentieth century carried out the project of realism and naturalism too well. They made the novel serve the function of documentation. Conversely, and Vargas Llosa has written on this many times, the modern novelist uses what the primitive novel documents—feelings, events, facts, etc.—to make art. As he says in *The Perpetual Orgy* "everything depends essentially on form, the deciding factor in determining whether a subject is beautiful or ugly, true false...the novelist must be above all else an artist, a tireless and incorruptible craftsman of style." The primitive novelist depended on plot and character to create mystery and suspense. The modernist uses narrative techniques like multiple viewpoints, vagueness, and nonlinear weavings of viewpoints to create a literary world.

In *The Time of the Hero,* Vargas Llosa successfully demonstrated his theory by weaving together four narrators into one plotline. By integrating the voices of Boa, Jaguar, Poet, and

Slave, a truer representation of life in the academy forms. By complicating the narrative technique, Vargas Llosa enables the structure of the story to bolster the plot. For example, by failing to identify Jaguar as one of the four, the judging of Jaguar remains impossible until he reveals himself to Lt. Gamboa. In other words, the narrative technique contains the power of the narration in the novel instead of giving it to the reader.

The technique of multiple perspectives utilizes the Faulknerian mode of nonlinear presentation. From the beginning, while the drama of the final two months at the academy unfolds, various flashbacks provide depth to the main characters as well as explanation to the importance of The Circle and the theft of an exam. The Slave has a flashback of moving; the Poet has a similar experience. Then there is a third flashback by an unidentified character which tricks the reader into believing it is either Slave or Poet. This confusion is not cleared up until the end. The confusion disallows an easy judgment of Jaguar. Instead, Jaguar, like Poet and Slave, reflects the environment of his upbringing. Using this technique bolsters the theme of secrecy as well as the confusing labyrinth of information each cadet masters according to the stature they have in their year. Jaguar, as undisputed master, even masters the narrative due to this secrecy as well as the lack of belief about the murder which accompanies his confession. Since the Poet has been favored as nearly a hero throughout the novel, the revelation that the Jaguar is the hero is not believable.

Plundering and Borrowing

In *Temptation of the World,* Efrain Kristal characterizes Vargas Llosa's literary technique "as a kind of amalgam of his own experience, literary works, other genres including cinema, and the research he has done around the world." It is no accident, therefore, that *The Time of the Hero* is rife with allusions and borrowings from other works. For example, a major influence on literature after World War II is existentialism and one novel in particular, *The Stranger* by Albert Camus, had a tremendous impact. Camus' novel concerns a murder committed by a man who found himself in a tense situation, bothered by the sunlight. Similarly, no one who has read Camus can miss the allusion to that famous Algerian murder scene when Jaguar beats a boy up for courting Teresa: "the sun broke into my head." There are obvious differences but the allusion is intentional.

Less recondite, the novel as a whole takes advantage, inexactly, of Vargas Llosa's own life experience. He was actually a student at the same military school. But that is where the resemblance ends. Instead, Vargas Llosa taps into an entire genre of boarding-school literature. Robert Musil's *Young Törless* also has a gang that tortures the weak and ends ambiguously. Another example of borrowing that looms over the entire work is the almost Oedipal family dynamic. Each character succeeds to the extent that he is able to overcome the emasculation his father performs on him. Jaguar's victory depends, in part, on the death of his parents.

The Poet has enough personal vitality to negotiate survival in the world outside his mother. The Slave never transitions from the world of the mother to that of the father. This is the source of his slave nature.

Such utilization of other works of art borders on the post-modern. As Vargas Llosa explains in *Perpetual Orgy*, "Imitation in literature is not a moral problem but an artistic one: all writers use, to varying degrees, forms that have been used before, but only those incapable of transforming these plagiarisms into something deserve to be called imitators." The success of the modern novel is its ability to stand on its own while also tapping into literature that is already transcendent of place and time. Camus' *The Stranger* was never confined, as a primitive novel would be, to Algeria and, therefore, allusion to the novel is safe, whereas, allusions to novels read only in Peru would be lost.

Literary Heritage

Colonial Literature and Independence

Although the conquistadors destroyed the libraries of the Inca, intellectuals of Indian and Spanish descent tried to recover as much as possible of pre-Conquest Peruvian literature. The most formidable of such efforts was undertaken by Garcilaso de la Vega—known as El Inca Garcilaso. By his mother's side he was of royal Inca heritage and Spanish by his father. He put together several volumes of Incan legends in Spanish.

When the Spanish finally left Latin America in 1830, writers dabbled with the techniques of Romanticism before adopting the form of the realist novel as the best vehicle for national literatures. These Spanish American novels, the "novelas de la tierra" or Regionalist novels, describe Latin American landscapes and rural life in exhaustive detail. Examples of such novels include *Dona Barbara* by Romul Gallegos or *The Vortex* by Jose Eustasio Rivera. Once this literature began to mix with indigenous myths and Latin American writers learned about the European avant-garde, a uniquely Latin American literature was born. The first generation of modernist Latin American writers created their techniques in Europe and then returned home. While Latin American modernism was forming, the nationalists were winning the culture wars. Nationalists promoted the regionalist style arguing that modernism was inappropriate.

Modernism

In Europe, the first generation of modernists made contact with each other, the European modernists and the avant-garde. Argentinean Jorge Luis Borges, Guatemalan Miguel Angel Asturias, and Cuban Alejo Carpentier studied the Mayan collections at the Sorbonne in Paris and the British Museum in London. In the former, they met the leading surrealists, Andre Breton and Paul Eluard, and in the latter made contact with the Bloomsbury Group. Other Latin American writers would join this nexus until, finally, Gabriel García Márquez, Carlos Fuentes, and the young Mario Vargas Llosa arrived. As a group, they praised William Faulkner, Marcel Proust, John Dos Passos, Franz Kafka, Gustave Flaubert, and Jean-Paul Sartre.

The heritage of the modern Latin American novel, therefore, sees its origins in the realists and not in the varied forms of the Enlightenment or the Romantics. The primitive novel, whether written by Charles Dickens or Victor Hugo, concerned itself with capturing the events of life. Eventually, the modernists—James Joyce and Virginia Woolf—revealed a way out. However, it took Flaubert and Faulkner to make use of the pathway and they inspired the generation of writers known as "El Boom," the greatest period of Spanish-language literature since Spain's seventeenth-century Golden Age.

The Boom

Throughout the 1940s Borges announced to Latin America that, contrary to the belief of the nationalists, literary invention is good. This enabled an awakening of creativity. García Márquez wrote under the influence of Borges and Faulkner. In the 1950s, Vargas Llosa had concluded that writing in the primitive, regionalist manner kept the Latin American novel Latin American. Following Borges and García Márquez, Vargas Llosa decided that the novel could be freed of this confinement when it ceased to be Latin American and began to be a literary world independent of the reader's possession of a Latin American experience. The key was to use the narrator and, through narrative techniques, to realize that authors do not record, but create.

Two forces assisted the new energy in Latin American fiction. First, the tough literary agent Carmen Balcells was on the lookout for Latin American fiction. Seix Barral, the most prestigious Spanish-language publishing firm, listened to Balcell. The American publishing house Harper and Row wanted to cash in on the buzz surrounding Latin American modernism and they were helped by a superb translator, Gregory Rabassa. The economic forces combined with the creative juices so that by the late 1950s, the boom began and everyone was reading fiction by Latin American authors.

Historical Context

Colonialism and Independence

During the sixteenth and seventeenth centuries, Lima, known to the Spanish as the City of Kings, served as the transition center for silver mined in the Andes and destined for Spain. With the fall of the Spanish Empire and the expiration of easily extractable silver, Lima declined. In the backcountry, the Indians were locked in a cycle of poverty that began with Spanish rule. Even in the 1990s, Indians form the peasant class of Peruvian society and Vargas Llosa notes a few of them in his book of 1962. The Indians are poor, malnourished, and during the 1990s wracked by cholera. Lima was renewed in the late nineteenth century when guano —bird droppings—were in demand due to their high concentrations of nitrogen, which is used in gunpowder. Peru had a huge supply of guano that it mined for the West. Chile, however, took the guano during the War of the Pacific (1879-1884) and Peru had to find other sources of economic sustenance.

Foreign investment helped Peru become a mercantile economy in the first half of the twentieth century. Peru exported copper, sugar, cotton, fishmeal, oil (until that too ran out), and wool. But as an export economy, Peru could not attract investors or create an industrial base. Therefore, much of its natural resources remained untapped;

recovering from centuries of colonial exploitation proved impossible. This changed when the Cold War began and the West became interested in Peru. Still, foreign investment and deforestation (a.k.a. economic growth) did not accelerate until the last quarter of the twentieth century.

General Odriá

During World War II, Peru, on the side of the Allies, only declared war against Japan and Germany in 1945 (in order to be a charter member of the United Nations). Peru's willingness to participate in world affairs and the onset of the Cold War brought Peru neo-imperialist attention from the U.S. In 1945, Jose Luis Bustamante y Rivero won the presidency of Peru representing a coalition of leftist parties including the American Popular Revolutionary Alliance (APRA). Part of their program included land reform for the Indians. This legitimately elected democratic government was not defended by the United Nations or the U.S. when General Manuel Odriá, supported by the oligarchy and military, overthrew them. For eight years, the corrupt and brutal regime of Odriá, who became president in 1950 though his opponent did not appear on the ballot, marginalized the socialist elements and increased defense spending rather than resolve Peru's long-standing problems. During Odriá's reign, university campuses were full of military spies and social mobility was tied to patriotic military service. Odriá's defense spending included an extension of its territorial waters. This move angered the U.S., whose fishing fleet regularly used those waters, but Peru exercised this extension in concert with Chile and Ecuador. The U.S. did little but protest. Peru, under Odriá, also initiated several cooperative pacts with Brazil. It is in this milieu that Vargas Llosa places his novel *The Time of the Hero.*

In 1956, Odriá allowed elections and lost to Manuel Prado y Ugarteche who had been president during World War II. Ostensible democratic rule continued; real power remained the domain of the forty families who formed the oligarchy with the support of the Catholic Church. During the next open elections, Victor Andres Belaunde won by promising economic reforms. In the meantime, the socialist left had been invigorated by the success of Fidel Castro's communist revolution in Cuba in 1959. It seemed possible to repeat Castro's success throughout Latin America. In 1965, tired of waiting for land reform, 300,000 Indians revolted. In response, the military, no longer willing to stand quietly behind the oligarchy, took over the government. By 1968, a military junta under General Juan Velasco Alvarado created a distinct pattern of Peruvian socialism. The military instituted land reforms. By 1975, the landowning elite had been destroyed and 40% of the land had been transferred to cooperative or peasant use. Economic downturns discredited the junta and Belaunde returned as president in 1980. His attempts to reverse the junta's programs led to widespread protests and the rise of the Shining Path.

Peru's Population

As the heartland of the ancient Inca Empire, it is not surprising to find that the most numerous segment of the approximately 25 million Peruvians is Native American (45 percent). Mestizos, those of mixed European (mostly Spanish) and Indian heritage, make up the next 37 percent. Those who consider themselves white make up 15 percent of the population, and the rest is split mostly between those of African and Japanese heritage. Because of historical circumstances, 90 percent of the people are Catholic, and Spanish remained the official language until 1975, when Quechua joined Spanish as the official languages of Peru.

Compare & Contrast

- **1960s:** In response to the Cuban Revolution, a force of U.S. CIA-trained Cuban exiles invade Cuba unsuccessfully in 1961 (an incident known as "the Bay of Pigs"). The U.S.S.R., to help defend its communist ally, tries to install missiles in Cuba. The U.S. refuses to allow the placement of missiles so close. The tense standoff in the fall of 1962 ends when the U.S. promises not to invade Cuba.

    Today: Although many governments have changed their

policies, the U.S. maintains a trade embargo on Cuba. Cuba, meanwhile, has outlived its larger communist ally, the Soviet Union, and has sought trade and reconciliation with anyone, including the Pope.

- **1960s:** Much of Latin America adopts import substitution industrialization (ISI) economic theory after World War I until the 1960s. This protectionist policy encourages domestic production of items otherwise imported. Political instability fostered by the neglect of land reform issues lead to its demise.

  Today: Fujimori, having defeated Shining Path and furthered Belaunde's privatization schemes, has made Peru friendly to foreign (especially Japanese and U.S.) investors. The economy has grown and the disparity between the rich and poor has increased.

- **1960s:** To stem the flow of people to the West, East German soldiers ripped up the streets on the night of April 13, 1961, and the Berlin Wall was born.

  Today: The Berlin Wall has been down since 1989 but the

reunification of Germany has proven costly and painful.

- **1960s:** Renegade priests throughout Latin America switched sides and began preaching 'liberation theology.' No longer supporters of the oligarchy, the priests sermonized against oppression of the poor and spoke favorably of Marxist reforms. Meanwhile, Pope John XXIII convened the Second Vatican Council to begin a reform of the Catholic Church.

Today: Catholicism is still strong in Latin America although as economic conditions improve for more people, its followers are secularizing. Pope John Paul II has made huge strides in reforming the church and in breaking down barriers between Catholicism, the Eastern Orthodox church, other sects of Christianity, Jews, and Muslims.

Economically, heritage means a great deal in Peru. Those who happen to have more European heritage also happen to claim more academic credentials and occupy the highest-paying jobs. These people make up the cream of Peruvian society and speak Spanish as well as another European language. By contrast, the Indians, who often do not speak Spanish let alone another European language, are relegated to peasant status, which borders on serfdom. They labor in agricultural industries or as sweatshop labor.

Just prior to embarking on his life in Europe, Vargas Llosa went on an anthropological expedition, visiting a tribe in the deep jungles of Peru. He was shocked, according to Rossman: "I discovered that Peru was not only a country of the twentieth century...but that Peru was also part of the Middle Ages and the Stone Age." He reflected on this disparity in his widely celebrated second novel, *The Green House.*

Shining Path

The plight of the Indian peasants and their unanswered plea for reform found a new champion in the 1980s in the form of a militant Maoist organization, the Shining Path. They laid siege to the government and in the ensuing conflict, some 15,000 people were "disappeared." Meanwhile, Peru's highland during the 1990s became the number-one production source for cocaine destined for the U.S. Alberto Fujimori, who defeated Vargas Llosa in the 1990 elections, used his popularity to assume emergency powers. Using ruthless military tactics in the face of terrorist acts and reprisals, Fujimori's military—with U.S. aid through the War on Drugs program—routed the forces of Shining Path. By 1992, the leader of Shining Path, Abimael Guzman, was in prison and Fujimori continued to pursue free-market economics.

Critical Overview

After reworking a mammoth 1500-page manuscript, Vargas Llosa found a publisher for *The Time of the Hero* with the most prestigious Hispanic publisher, Seix Barral of Barcelona. When the novel came out in 1963, having already been awarded one literary prize, Vargas Llosa proved that the recent international attention focused on Latin American fiction had not been misplaced. In Latin America, the novel—unlike many internationally acclaimed novels—was an instant bestseller. Critical reception has been wholly enthusiastic and ranges from appreciation for the subtlety of Vargas Llosa's social critique to his ability to utilize modernist techniques and further "El Boom." Some critics credit Vargas Llosa's novel with moving the boom in Latin American literature into its second wave. Carlos Fuentes heralded the boom with his 1958 novel, *Where the Air Is Clear,* and García Márquez's 1967 novel, *One Hundred Years of Solitude,* marked the start of the final wave.

In his acceptance speech for an award for *The Green House* in 1967, Vargas Llosa postulated that the writer is under obligation to help society improve by airing its dirty laundry. He believes that by exposing human failings in fictional form, people can better see what they need to do. As Charles Rossman says in "Mario Vargas Llosa's *The Green House:* Modernist Novel from Peru," Vargas Llosa has always felt this way but *The Time of the Hero* "neither conveys a simple, didactic message nor recommends an explicit course of action." Still, Vargas Llosa's first novel was a huge success and more than verified his authorial theory: he had exposed military culture and they responded in kind.

"One thousand copies were ceremoniously burned in the patio of the school and several generals attacked it bitterly. One of them said that the book was the work of a 'degenerate mind,' and another, who was more imaginative, claimed that I had undoubtedly been paid by Ecuador to undermine the prestige of the Peruvian Army," Vargas Llosa recalls in a *New York Times* article, "A Passion for Peru." While the military was busy vilifying Vargas Llosa, critics were in raptures over the technical, specifically narrative, sophistication of the work. Jose Miguel Oviedo explores the prescience of Vargas Llosa's insight into the role of the military, showing that the author reveals the way in which military life "reproduce[s] itself, deformed and monstrous, on the other side of the social body. What allowed the military to survive destroyed the essence of civilian life, asphyxiating it under the hateful norms of imposition and supremacy that many times have been singled out as great regulators in the narrative world of Vargas Llosa." For Oviedo, the revelation of this insight makes the novel a moral one.

J. J. Armas Marcelo explains how Vargas Llosa uses secrecy as a technique to expose the military hegemony Oviedo sees exposed. Oviedo's two sides of society become, in Marcelo, the world of appearance and the world of secrecy. "These two worlds are within the same forge of the narrative structure of the work, shaping, to a greater or lesser degree, the symmetry or asymmetry of the elements that constitute the novelistic whole." Not only does Vargas Llosa expose military culture but he immerses the reader in that culture by employing secrecy and ambiguity around the central crime in the novel.

Other critics have picked up on the bipolarity of Peruvian society as presented by Vargas Llosa. The novel, writes D. P. Gallagher, "is never better than when it is showing how for young Peruvians social intercourse presupposes the jettisoning of one's best instincts." Raymond Williams says, "The plot and structure makes inevitable an awareness of Peruvian society and a judgment of the characters' actions." Williams adds that Vargas Llosa's techniques successfully force "adjustments in the reading process to understand…temporarily suspending traditional assumptions about" how novels work. Sara Castro-Klaren notes that Vargas Llosa's characterization technique mimics the chivalric tale where characters "often act under an assumed name or a disguised identity." The disguise, subsequently, turns out to be a truer representation of the character's real self. Thus, we remember Jaguar as the kingpin and not as the kind man offering to help an old friend.

Because of the candid way Vargas Llosa has admitted to being influenced by European existential writers as well as writers of the American South, critics have often attempted to make comparisons. Efrain Kristal compares *The Time of the Hero* to William Faulkner's *Light in August,* one of Vargas Llosa's favorites. Like Faulkner, Vargas Llosa's plot hinges on the revelation of "a hidden fact at a particularly timely moment." R. Z. Sheppard says that García Márquez is Faulkner while Vargas Llosa is "aesthetically, if not stylistically, [Peru's] Dreiser" and his first novel "was a brutal slab of naturalism."

There were some negative reviews. Luis Harss and Barbara Dohmann characterize *The Time of the Hero* as obsessively "realist." They view the novel as "a desperate search for wholeness. A sort of vicarious return to the womb of a lost reality." Despite this early review, Vargas Llosa enjoys a positive reputation even though his subsequent works have not been ceremoniously burned. John Updike explains this continued favor, noting that "the Peruvian man of letters, Mario Vargas Llosa, is almost too good to be true; cosmopolitan, handsome, and versatile, he puts a pleasant face on the Latin American revolution in the novel, and… makes everybody, even North Americans, feel better about being a writer."

What Do I Read Next?

- In his second novel, *La casa verde* (1966; translation by Gregory Rabassa published as *The Green House* 1968), Vargas Llosa again took experiences from his own life and created a work about the whole of Peru. His visit with an Amazonian tribe as part of an anthropological expedition as well as his experience of a brothel in the town of Piura establish the basis for a meeting of two ends of Peruvian culture that seldom occurs. The novel begins when two nuns and a sergeant with his helpers steal two girls from the Aguaruna tribe but the girls escape.

- Vargas Llosa's acceptance speech in

1967 for an award for *Green House* has been published as *La literatura es fuego (Literature Is Fire)*. In this speech, Vargas Llosa summarized his view of the writer. He said that the writer has an obligation to assist his society in whatever way he can. For him, this means that the writer must engage in constructive criticism with the society he inhabits.

- *Conversacion en la catedral* (1969; translation by Rabassa published as *Conversation in the Cathedral,* 1975) is the story of Santiago Zavala. Much like Vargas Llosa's other males, Santiago is expected to follow in his father's footsteps. The opposite happens when Santiago chooses to fraternize with the lower class in order to escape the corruption of his father's social group.

- Vargas Llosa underwent an artistic transition which is revealed in his 1973 novel, *Pantaleon y las visitadoras* (published as *Captain Pantoja and the Special Service,* 1978). While the artistic technique differs from the novels of the 1960s, the themes are familiar: the military and corruption. Captain Pantaleon

Pantoja has been given special orders to go undercover and establish a prostitution ring to serve soldiers at the front. The army hopes to end rapes on civilian women in this way but they cannot be connected with trafficking in female flesh, so Pantoja cannot tell anybody who he really is.

- Using a bit of his own biography, Vargas Llosa's 1977 novel, *La tia Julia y el escribidor* (translated as *Aunt Julia and the Scriptwriter*, 1982), concerns a novelist who falls in love with his aunt. This novel explores, with humor, the struggles of the creative process.

- One of Vargas Llosa's most recent novels, *Death in the Andes* (1996), involves the Shining Path movement, Dionysian rituals, a witch, human sacrifice, mystery, and Peruvian society. The storyline focuses on the disappearance of three men from a village and the soldiers who investigate. The tale turns into a murder mystery and a panoramic depiction of late-twentieth-century Peru.

- The German academies of the early twentieth century served as the model for such institutions as the

Leoncio Prado Academy. Robert Musil's novel *Young Torless* reveals the psychological torment boys inflict on each other in such high-stress academies. Although the protagonists are dismissed as mere boys, their mentality and behavior are not dissimilar from those of the army officers they revere.

- British schoolboys are just as capable of living out male fantasies as German, Peruvian, or American boys. William Golding said as much in his classic novel, *Lord of the Flies.* A nuclear war leads to the evacuation of Britain and a planeload of prep-school boys crashes on an island. Once there, the boys form two gangs and the gang representing primitive nature would have won had the adult rescuers been any later.

- The pressure placed on young men of the upper classes by their fathers is enormous, even in America. In *The Dead Poets Society,* by N. H. Kleinbaum and Stephen Haft (1989), rich boys are schooled in a stuffy atmosphere until a new English teacher, Mr. Keating, turns them on to great poets like Walt Whitman. They are so excited about literature as a result that they begin to break the rules in order to read poetry or to pursue love. Neil Perry would rather kill himself than live in his father's world where everything is serious and being an actor in a Shakespearean drama is outlawed.

Sources

Castro-Klaren, Sara, *Understanding Mario Vargas Llosa,* University of South Carolina Press, 1990.

Gallagher, D. P., "Mario Vargas Llosa," Oxford University Press, 1973, pp. 122-43.

Gerdes, Dick, *"The Time of the Hero* : Lost Innocence," in *Mario Vargas Llosa,* Twayne Publishers, 1985, pp. 33-52.

Harss, Luis, and Barbara Dohmann, "Mario Vargas Llosa, or The Revolving Door," in their *Into the Mainstream: Conversations with Latin-American Writers,* Harper, 1967, pp. 342-75.

Kristal, Efrain, *Temptation of the Word: The Novels of Mario Vargas Llosa,* Vanderbilt University Press, 1998.

Marcelo, J. J. Armas, "Secrecy: A Structural Concept of *The Time of the Hero,'"* in *World Literature Today,* translated by Mary E. Davis, Vol. 52, No. 1, Winter, 1978, pp. 68-70.

Oviedo, Jose Miguel, "The Theme of the Traitor and the Hero: On Vargas Llosa's Intellectuals and the Military," translated by Richard A. Valdes, in *World Literature Today,* Vol. 52, No. 1, Winter, 1978, pp. 16-24.

Rossman, Charles, "Mario Vargas Llosa's *The Green House:* Modernist Novel from Peru," in *The Modernists, Studies in a Literary Phenomenon:*

Essays in Honor of Harry T. Moore, edited by Lawrence B. Gamache and Ian S. MacNiven, Farleigh Dickinson University Press, 1987, pp. 261-74.

Sheppard, R. Z., "Caged Condor," in *Time,* February 17, 1975, pp. E3, 84.

Vargas Llosa, Mario, "A Passion for Peru," in *New York Times Magazine,* November 20, 1983, pp. 106, 108.

———, *The Perpetual Orgy: Flaubert and Madame Bovary,* translated by Helen Lane, Farrar, Straus, 1986.

Williams, Raymond Leslie, "The Beginnings," in *Mario Vargas Llosa,* Ungar, 1986, pp. 19-38.

Further Reading

Allende, Isabel, *Of Love and Shadows,* Bantam Books, 1988.

> Allende brings a feminist challenge to both the masculine world of Latin America and the Boom. *Of Love and Shadows* takes place in a Latin American country gripped by a military dictator. A wealthy woman, Irene Beltran, and a Spanish exile's son, Francisco Leal, fall in love but discover a crime which puts their lives at risk.

Bronte, Charlotte, *Jane Eyre,* Scholastic Paperbacks, 1996.

> One of the first novels to investigate the struggles of a youth against circumstances is Bronte's *Jane Eyre* (originally published in 1847). Jane struggles through a boarding-school situation where there is a hint of some of the physical abuses associated with twentieth-century boarding-school stories.

Ehrenreich, Barbara, *Blood Rites: Origins and History of the Passions of War,* Henry Holt, 1998.

> Ehrenreich, who wrote the foreword to the University of Minnesota Press

edition of Theweleit's *Male Fantasies,* has been a leading contributor to American histories of sexuality. In *Blood Rites,* Ehrenreich argues that humans developed war to deal with the anxieties of self-consciously being a part of the food chain. This argument is then used as a foundation to explain why modern efforts to achieve peace are so difficult.

Fuentes, Carlos, *Where the Air Is Clear,* Noonday Press, 1971.

The first novel of El Boom, Fuentes' 1958 story indicts Mexican society by discussing its post-revolutionary reality. An epic of Mexico City urban history, Fuentes weaves together the biographies of zany characters—including an Aztec god—to unlock the Mexican psyche.

García Márquez, Gabriel, *One Hundred Years of Solitude,* Harperperennial Library, 1998.

Perhaps the most famous novel of the Latin American Boom, García Márquez's 1967 masterpiece perfected the magical realism style. The novel records the history of post-colonial Latin America through the fantastic struggles of the Buendia family.

Gibson, James William, *Warrior Dreams: Violence and Manhood in Post-Vietnam America,* Hill and Wang, 1994.

> Gibson goes undercover to visit gun camps and affiliates of militia groups. He finds military and fascist fantasies lurk in the hidden compounds of these far-right groups even in America.

Oviedo, Jose Miguel, "The Theme of the Traitor and the Hero: On Vargas Llosa's Intellectuals and the Military," translated by Richard A. Valdes, in *World Literature Today,* Vol. 52, No. 1, Winter, 1978, pp. 16-24.

> Oviedo discusses the consistency with which Vargas Llosa employs the dichotomy of intellectual and military men in his fiction. The regularity with which this theme occurs leads Oviedo to conclude that this dichotomy is important to Peruvian culture and to Vargas Llosa personally. Somehow, this dichotomy must be resolved peaceably since both are intrinsic to Peru's culture.

Puig, Manuel, *Kiss of the Spider Woman,* edited by Erroll McDonald, translated by Thomas Colchie, Vintage Books, 1991.

> Originally published in 1976 as *El beso de la mujer arana, Kiss of the*

> *Spider Woman* remains the most famous novel by Puig—a member of the Boom generation condemned in his home country of Argentina for his overt homosexuality. Two men are holding a conversation in jail: the first is Molina, an apolitical homosexual; the other is Valentin, a young socialist revolutionary outraged by Molina's sexuality. By the end of the novel, they have fallen in love and switched places and perspectives.

Swanson, Philip, *The New Novel in Latin America,* Manchester University Press, 1995.

> Swanson analyzes the Boom in Latin American literature by showing how it came about and who the major figures were. This account takes away the surprise of the Boom by showing who influenced Fuentes, Vargas Llosa, and García Márquez.

Theweleit, Klaus, *Male Fantasies,* Polity Press, 1987.

> Theweleit examines the papers and libraries of leading Friekorpsmen to expose the sexual tensions which accompanied their warrior ideology. He places their sexual politics in the context of Fascism and its heritage of the European history of sexuality.

Vargas Llosa, Mario, *Pez, en el agua (A Fish in the Water: A Memoir),* Farrar Straus & Giroux, 1994.

> Vargas Llosa records his experience as a presidential candidate and reflects on his life. He tells of the disgusting nature of back-stabbing that accompanies political campaigning as well as the story of his journey from boy to man.

Milton Keynes UK
Ingram Content Group UK Ltd.
UKHW022213281223
435132UK00009B/390

Milton Keynes UK
Ingram Content Group UK Ltd.
UKHW022213281223
435132UK00009B/390